An Invitation to Tea

Emilie Barnes

with art by

Sandy Lynam Clough

HARVEST HOUSE PUBLISHERS
Eugene, Oregon 97402

An Invitation to Tea

Copyright ©1996 Harvest House Publishers
Eugene, OR 97402

ISBN 1-56507-462-9

All works of art reproduced in this book are copyrighted by Sandy Lynam Clough and may not be copied or reproduced without the artist's permission. Information regarding art prints featured in this book: Sandy Clough Studio, 25 Trail Road, Marietta, GA 30064

Text is taken from *If Teacups Could Talk* by Emilie Barnes (Harvest House Publishers, 1994).

Art direction, design and production by Garborg Design Works, Minneapolis, Minnesota.

Printed in Hong Kong.

06 / NG / 12 11 10

CONTENTS

Come and share

———

a pot of tea,

———

My home is warm

———

and

———

my friendship's free.

An Invitation to Tea

When did you last have a tea party? When was the last time you enjoyed a cup of tea with someone you care about? Isn't it time you did again?

Perhaps you have had the privilege of "taking tea" in the grand British style at a distinguished old country inn or a pretty little tea shop. All over the country, people are rediscovering the civilized joys of a traditional afternoon tea, with its elegant settings and its dainty sandwiches, its meticulously arranged platters of luscious sweets and perfectly brewed cups of tea. With a little care and a minimum of expense, you can enjoy this lovely ritual in your own home.

Or perhaps the idea of a tea party takes you back to childhood. Do you remember dressing up and putting on your best manners as you sipped pretend tea out of tiny cups and shared pretend delicacies with your friends, your parents, or your teddy bears? Were you lucky enough to have adults who cared enough to share tea parties with you? And are you lucky enough to have a little person with whom you could share a tea party today? Is there a little girl inside you who longs for a lovely time of childish imagination and "so big" manners?

It could be that the mention of teatime brings quieter memories—cups of amber liquid sipped in peaceful solitude on a big old porch, or friendly confidences shared over steaming cups.

But even if you don't care for tea—if you prefer coffee or cocoa or lemonade or ice water, or if you like chunky mugs better than gleaming silver or delicate china, or if you find the idea of a traditional tea overly formal and a bit intimidating— there's still room for you at the tea table. Few can resist a tea party when it is served with the right spirit.

You see, it's not the tea itself that speaks to the soul with such a satisfying message. And it's not the teacups them- selves that bring such a message of beauty and serenity and friendship.

It's not the tea, in other words, that makes the teatime special. It's the spirit of the tea party.

It's what happens when women or men or children make a place in their lives for the rituals of sharing. It's what happens when we bother with the little extras that feed the soul and nurture the senses and make space for unhurried conversa- tion. And when that happens, it doesn't really matter what fills the cups or holds the liquid.

It really isn't the tea.

It's the spirit of the tea party.

And, it is in that spirit I offer an invitation to tea.

Just for Me

A SOLITARY TEA

You don't need a lot of people to enjoy a lovely tea party. Taking the time to prepare a lovely tea just for you will calm you down and give you a wonderfully pampered feeling. Why not take a break in a long afternoon to enjoy a quiet cup in a lovely spot? Or if you have the luxury of an evening to yourself, why not prepare tea with fruit and sandwiches around five o'clock and then not worry about dinner? You'll have more time to enjoy the evening, and you'll sleep better because you ate early and light.

Here's a simple menu for a solitary tea that is easy to prepare, healthful, and satisfying.

A Perfect Pot of Tea (see instructions on page 9)
Orange or Apple Slices or a Beautiful Bunch of Grapes
Cream Cheese, Celery & Walnut Sandwiches
Homemade or Store-Bought Cookies

While waiting for the water to boil and the tea to steep, prepare one or more sandwiches and arrange them on a plate with the fruit and cookies. Lay a pretty cloth on a tray or on the table and add a flower or a candle for elegance. Then sit down at the table or carry your tray to a cozy spot. Enjoy!

CREAM CHEESE, CELERY AND WALNUT SANDWICHES

This easy-to-do filling can be made in minutes.

- ¼ pound cream cheese, room temperature
- ¼ celery heart, very finely chopped
- ¼ cup diced walnuts
- White or whole-wheat bread
- Parsley sprigs (for garnish)

In a small bowl, beat cream cheese until smooth. Mix in celery and walnuts. Make sandwiches with cheese mixture. Trim off crusts of bread and cut sandwiches into rectangles or triangles. Garnish plate with sprigs of parsley.

BREWING A PERFECT POT OF TEA

Preparing a perfect cup of tea takes time! But these simple steps can make the difference between a mediocre cup of tea and an excellent one.

1. Empty the teakettle and refill it with freshly drawn cold water. Put the kettle on to boil.

2. While the kettle is heating, pour hot water into the teapot to warm it. Ceramic (china, porcelain, stoneware) or glass teapots work best; tea brewed in a metal teapot may have a metallic taste.

3. Pour the hot water out of the teapot and add the tea. Measure a spoonful of loose tea for each cup desired into the warmed (empty) teapot, plus one extra spoonful for the pot. (Most teapots hold five to six cups.) If you are using teabags, use one bag less than the desired number of cups. Put the lid back on the pot until the water boils.

4. As soon as the kettle comes to a rolling boil, remove from heat. Overboiling causes the water to lose oxygen, and the resulting brew will taste flat.

5. Pour boiling water into the teapot and let the tea brew from three to six minutes. Small tea leaves will take less time to brew than large ones.

6. Gently stir the tea before pouring it through a tea strainer into the teacups. If you used teabags, remove them.

Of all the things which

wisdom provides to

make life entirely happy,

much the greatest is the

possession of friendship.

—EPICURUS

Cream Tea for Two

A ONE-ON-ONE PARTY WITH A SPECIAL FRIEND

*S*cones are the staple delicacy of an English tea. Simple and delicious, they resemble a giant, flaky, slightly sweet biscuit. In England they are pronounced to rhyme with *lawn* not *cone*—but however you say the word, scones are wonderful!

In England, a cream tea is one in which the traditional scones are served with clotted cream or Devonshire cream instead of butter. You cannot find the same kind of cream in the United States (our cows and our milk delivery system are different), but there are many possible substitutes. So why not invite a special friend over to enjoy a special one-on-one cream tea with you? This would be a great way to celebrate a birthday or to say thank you.

The key to making this one-on-one tea memorable is to plan and prepare for it just as carefully as you would a tea party for ten. Write out an invitation on a pretty card and send it to your friend, and allow plenty of time to decorate your table and prepare the food.

Tangerine Special Tea
Scones with Butter
Strawberry Preserves, Homemade or Otherwise
Clotted Cream

Buy or pick out two "companion" flowers—two roses, two carnations, two daffodils—and arrange in a vase with ferns or baby's breath. Spread a lovely tea cloth on a table or a tray, and use the very nicest pot and cups you have. Light a candle and set a little gift (a card, a book, a tape, a small decorative object, something you've made) at your friend's place. Put on his or her favorite kind of music. Dress up. Let your time together feel out of the ordinary without being stiff. And use this time to say the kinds of things you may not have shared before—just how much your special friend means to you.

TANGERINE SPECIAL TEA

4 tangerine slices
12 whole cloves
4 sticks of cinnamon
2 tablespoons sugar
4 cups orange pekoe tea
    brewed with the rind of
    one tangerine

Stud each slice of tangerine with 3 cloves. Now place a tangerine slice, a cinnamon stick, and 1½ teaspoons sugar in each cup. Fill with hot tea from the pot. Serve, using the cinnamon stick to stir the tea. Recipe makes 4 cups—plenty for two people.

BASIC SCONES

Scones are quite simple to make, so I usually make my own. However, a packaged scone mix can also give you very good results. You can add all kinds of extras to scones, depending on your taste. Try cut-up apples, currants, ginger, orange, almond flavoring, cinnamon, apricots, fresh blueberries, cranberries, or even chocolate chips.

2 cups flour
1 tablespoon baking powder
2 tablespoons sugar
½ teaspoon salt

6 tablespoons butter
½ cup buttermilk
Lightly beaten egg

Mix dry ingredients. Cut in 6 tablespoons butter until mixture resembles coarse cornmeal. Make a well in the center and pour in buttermilk. If you don't have buttermilk, use regular milk. Mix until dough clings together and is a bit sticky—do not overmix. Turn out dough onto a floured surface and shape into a 6- to 8-inch round about 1½ inches thick. Quickly cut into pie wedges or use a large round biscuit cutter to cut circles. The secret of tender scones is a minimum of handling. Place on ungreased cookie sheet, being sure the sides of scones don't touch each other. Brush with egg for a shiny, beautiful brown scone. Bake at 425° for 10 to 20 minutes, or until light brown.

· · · · · · · · ·

CLOTTED CREAM

Either of these two recipes makes an acceptable substitute for English clotted cream. In a pinch, you can also use commercial whipped topping.

Sue's Crème Fraîche
1 cup heavy cream
1 tablespoon buttermilk

Combine the cream and buttermilk in a saucepan over medium heat. Heat just until the chill is off—to about 90°. Pour into a glass jar, cover lightly with a piece of waxed paper, and let set in a warm place (65-70°) for 12 to 20 hours, until thickened. Replace the waxed paper with plastic wrap or a tight-fitting lid and refrigerate for at least 6 hours. (It will keep about two weeks in the refrigerator.) You can whip this substance to make it thicker or add a little sugar if you like your cream sweet.

Mock Devonshire Cream
½ cup heavy cream or
    8 ounces softened cream
    cheese
2 tablespoons confectioners'
    sugar
½ cup sour cream

In a chilled bowl, beat cream until medium-stiff peaks form, adding sugar during the last few minutes of beating. (If you are using cream cheese, just stir together with sugar.) Fold in sour cream and blend. Makes 1½ cups.

A hardened and

shameless tea-drinker...

who with tea amuses

the evening, with tea

solaces the midnight,

and with tea welcomes

the morning.

—SAMUEL JOHNSON

The Proper Way

A TRADITIONAL VICTORIAN AFTERNOON TEA

Not all your tea parties have to follow the guidelines of traditional etiquette, but I urge you to try a traditional afternoon tea at least once. In my experience, those who sample a traditional Victorian afternoon tea find it absolutely delightful!

Begin your planning with an invitation. In Victorian days the invitations were beautifully engraved on white paper. Today almost anything goes—even a phone call. But there is something about a written invitation that honors a guest—as well as providing her with a written reminder of the date and time of the occasion. Printed invitations on lovely white paper are still a charming touch for a tea party. A printed border of roses or pansies is also appropriate, and so are "tea" note cards.

The wording should be simple and clear:

An Invitation to Tea

Emilie Barnes requests the pleasure of your company for afternoon tea. Saturday, July 9 between three and five o'clock. R.S.V.P.

Once the invitations are out, turn your thoughts to preparing the table. Traditional tea parties call for a lovely white cloth of linen, lace, or crisp cotton. In a pinch you can use a clean white sheet and dress it up with white doilies. You will also need white linen or cotton serviettes (napkins) for each person.

The centerpiece is normally a fresh bouquet of roses and greenery, or a bunch of daisies and baby's breath will also do. Don't get hung up on decorations; in a traditional afternoon tea, the food is the real centerpiece. I do love to use a few candles or oil lamps on my tea table to add romance and warmth.

Next, get out all your pretty serving pieces, the ones you never use—Grandma's teapot, teacups, silver tray, other silver pieces, china plates. What if you don't have all these collected and inherited lovelies? Use what you have—even if it is only paper goods—or borrow from friends. The proper "equipment" adds that special touch to a formal afternoon tea, but don't let the lack of it keep you from experiencing the fun of a tea party.

If you enjoy your tea, you can then begin collecting the proper accoutrements. Over the years, in addition to all my teacups, I have collected special dishes, silver teapots, lovely trays, and crisp linens for my tea parties. Many were forgotten treasures I uncovered at garage or estate sales. When one of my aunts died, I inherited many of her pretty things that are perfect for my tea parties.

Look in antique shops or thrift shops for china, silver, and linen. Let friends and family know you'd love "tea things" for birthdays or Christmas—a single silver spoon, dainty tongs for serving lumps of sugar, a bone-china teacup or teapot, a damask linen cloth. These are heirlooms you will one day pass down to the next generation. They will also motivate you to have more tea parties!

Once your table is arranged and your guests have arrived, you'll want to serve your tea in the proper way.

The cream goes first into the cups. Yes, the English use cream in their tea, although it's really milk. The tannins in strong black tea will cause real cream to curdle, so milk is used but called cream. The sugar—in cube form only, please—goes in next.

Of course, you will ask your guests ahead of time whether they want cream or sugar. Some will ask for two lumps, and children may ask for as many as six! The sugar cubes go into the cups and then, finally, the brewed tea. Be sure to pour the tea slowly; fill the cup but don't pour in so much as to cause a spill. A silver teaspoon, usually a tiny one, is used to stir the tea. I use my children's silver-plated baby spoons for stirring; these make wonderful conversation pieces.

For guests who don't care for tea but still want to join the teatime festivities, consider serving punch in a beautiful cut-glass bowl. This is a long-standing English tradition.

Our menu for afternoon tea will be a traditional array of tender scones, dainty tea sandwiches, and luscious sweets:

Darjeeling or Assam Tea
Scones with Clotted Cream and Lemon Curd
Tea Sandwiches
Trifle Fit for a Queen
Emilie's Triple Chocolate Fudge Cake

LEMON CURD

Lemon curd, sometimes called lemon cheese, is a very common English preserve. It is used as a spread for sandwiches, muffins, crumpets and so forth, and it also makes a delicious tart filling.

Grated peel of 4 lemons
Juice of 4 lemons (about 1 cup)
4 eggs, beaten
½ cup butter, cut in small pieces
2 cups sugar

In the top of a large double boiler, combine lemon peel, lemon juice, eggs, butter, and sugar. Place over simmering water and stir until sugar is dissolved. Continue to cook, stirring occasionally, until thickened and smooth. While hot, pour into hot, sterilized ½-pint canning jars, leaving about ⅛ inch for headspace. Run a narrow spatula down between lemon curd and side of jar to release air. Top with sterilized lids; firmly screw on bands. Place in a draft-free area to cool and store in a cool, dry place. (I keep in the refrigerator.) Lemon curd doesn't keep indefinitely, so make only as much as you will use in a couple of weeks. Makes about 1 pint.

TEA SANDWICHES

Afternoon tea sandwiches are made from very thinly sliced bread with crusts removed. Spread bread with unsalted butter, herb butter, mayonnaise, or cream cheese. Add filling and cut into squares, rectangles, or diamond shapes–or use cookie cutters for round or heart-shaped sandwiches. Tea sandwiches may be made ahead, covered with a damp tea towel or plastic wrap, and refrigerated until serving time. Decorate serving trays with fresh flowers or herbs.

CUCUMBER SANDWICHES are perhaps most commonly associated with afternoon tea. Peel cucumbers and slice very thin. Sprinkle slices with salt and drain on paper towels. Spread white bread with unsalted butter and a thin layer of cream cheese and layer cucumbers no more than ¼ inch high. Cut into desired shapes.

WATERCRESS SANDWICHES are also favorite tea-party fare. Butter white or rye bread and fill with watercress leaves. Cut into squares, arrange on plate, and garnish with watercress.

OTHER TEA SANDWICH IDEAS:
- Thinly sliced chicken breast or smoked salmon with watercress and mayonnaise on white bread.
- Bagel rounds (slice one bagel in thirds horizontally). Spread with cream cheese and topped with thin slices of smoked salmon, tomato rounds, minced onions, and capers.
- Stilton cheese crumbled over apple slices on pumpernickel bread.

- Cream cheese mixed with chutney, a dash of curry, and lemon juice on white bread.
- Paper-thin slices of red radish on white bread spread with unsalted butter.
- Tomato slices sprinkled with freshly chopped basil on rye bread spread with mayonnaise.

TRIFLE FIT FOR A QUEEN

Trifle is a wonderful English dish, perfect for tea!

5 peaches, peeled and sliced
⅔ cup plus 2 tablespoons peach schnapps
One 5 x 9 inch pound cake, purchased or homemade
Fresh berries for garnish
10 ladyfingers
1 recipe Peach Cream (recipe follows)
1 cup whipping cream
2 tablespoons sugar

Brush flat sides of ladyfingers with ⅓ cup of peach schnapps and line the sides and bottom of a glass serving bowl with 8 to 10 cup capacity. Spoon half of the Peach Cream over the ladyfingers lining the bottom of the dish. Arrange half of the peaches on top of the Peach Cream. Slice cake lengthwise into ½ inch slices and brush cake slices on both sides with ⅓ cup schnapps. Arrange half of the cake slices on top of peaches. Repeat layers of Peach Cream, peaches, and cake slices. Whip cream until medium soft peaks form. Add sugar and 2 tablespoons schnapps and continue beating until blended. Spread cream mixture over the top of trifle and garnish with fresh berries. Wrap tightly with plastic wrap and refrigerate overnight. Makes 8 servings.

PEACH CREAM

8 egg yolks
2¼ cups half-and-half
3 tablespoons peach schnapps
6 tablespoons sugar
4 teaspoons cornstarch

In a medium bowl beat egg yolks until thickened. Gradually add sugar and beat until mixture is thick and lemon colored. Pour into a saucepan and beat in 2 cups half-and-half. Mix cornstarch with remaining half-and-half and beat into egg mixture. Cook over medium-low heat and stir constantly until mixture thickens (6 to 8 minutes). Do not let mixture boil. Remove from heat and stir in the peach schnapps. Cool to room temperature and then chill. Mixture will thicken more as it cools.

EMILIE'S TRIPLE CHOCOLATE FUDGE CAKE

This is so easy and so good, a hit with every bite! You may want to have it at every tea party!

1 small package chocolate pudding mix (not instant)
1 box chocolate cake mix (dry mix)
½ cup semisweet chocolate pieces
½ cup chopped nuts
Whipped cream

Cook pudding as directed on package and blend dry cake mix into hot pudding. (Mixture will be thick.) Pour into prepared oblong pan (13 x 9½ x 2 inches) and sprinkle with chocolate pieces and nuts. Bake 30 to 35 minutes at 350°. Cool 5 minutes, cut into 2-inch squares, and arrange on cake plate or doily-lined tray. Serve plain or topped with a dollop of whipped cream.

When you and your dollies

So festive and jolly

Sit down to your afternoon tea,

Since I can't come tripping

To join in your sipping,

Please drink a wee cupful for me.

—NINETEENTH CENTURY GREETING CARD

All Dressed Up

A GROWNUP PARTY
FOR CHILDREN

hildren love to play dress-up, and they love to have tea. So gather a group of your favorite little people for this special party. Children can be anywhere from about four to ten or eleven, but you will have to adjust your activities to the age group. A group of three to five children is a manageable number, or invite children with their parents.

And don't assume that a tea like this is just for girls. Most little boys, in my experience, relish their own special teatimes, and the adults who bother to ask them to tea end up learning a lot about the children and themselves.

Let the children (or the little host or hostess) help with as much of the preparation as possible; older children can do a lot of it themselves. Buy or make some pretty cards for invitations, or let the children make them. (Be sure the basic facts are there—and readable!)

Spend some time before the day of the party hunting up dress-up clothes—hats, scarves, jewelry, gloves, handbags, artificial flowers. You might find that a trip to the thrift shop (or an older relative) yields many treasures for very little money.

Allow at least half an hour before the tea goes on the table for everyone to dress up. (If grownups are part of this party, they should dress up too.)

The menu for this children's party was put together with the help of a child! Children love petits fours—the little cakes are just their size—and you can get them from almost any bakery. If you can't find them and don't want to make them, just serve an assortment of small cookies. The cream-cheese mints are very easy and fun for children to make.

Pink Tea (Pink Lemonade or Strawberry Herbal Tea)
Party Pinwheels or Simple Tea Sandwiches
Strawberries with Confectioners' Sugar for Dipping
Petits Fours or Cookie Assortment
Cream Cheese Mints

PARTY PINWHEELS

1-pound loaf of unsliced
  day-old white bread
  (fresh bread will be
  difficult to cut)
½ cup unsalted butter,
  room temperature
Filling of your choice
  (I like plain cream
  cheese sprinkled with
  paprika, but you could
  also use egg salad, tuna,
  or any other soft filling—
  even peanut butter!)

Neatly cut off all crusts
from loaf of bread. Lightly
spread butter to edges of
one long side. Cut lengthwise into as thin a slice as
possible. Spread buttered
side of slice with filling. Roll
up lengthwise, jelly-roll
style. Wrap in foil. Repeat
until loaf is finished—you
should have about 6 rolls.
Refrigerate for at least an
hour; butter will harden and
hold rolls together. Before
serving, cut each roll cross-
wise in about 5 slices.
Makes about 30 pinwheels.

CREAM CHEESE MINTS

2¼ cups confectioners'
  sugar
3 ounces softened cream
  cheese
Peppermint flavoring to
  taste (about ¼ tea-
  spoon)
Food coloring
Granulated sugar
Candy molds (optional)

Mash cheese and mix in
sugar. If you will be using
more than one color,
divide mixture and place in
separate bowls. Add flavoring and color sparingly;
you want soft pastels with
a delicate flavor. Stir
together until mixture
resembles pie dough. Roll
into small balls and roll
each ball in granulated
sugar. Press balls into pat-
ties with glass dipped in
granulated sugar or press
them into candy molds and
unmold at once. (Shake
sugar into mold, if neces-
sary, to prevent sticking.)

To many a youth,

and many a maid,

Dancing in the

chequered shade.

And young and old

come forth to play.

On a sunshine holiday.

—JOHN MILTON

A Teddy Bear Tea

A CHILD'S PARTY
FOR GROWNUPS

*W*ho doesn't sometimes long to be a child again? Even people who "never had a childhood" may wax nostalgic for the days when imagination ruled and the biggest decision of the day was "What shall I play now?" A teddy bear tea for grownups can be both poignant and enchanting.

If you can, send invitations on teddy-bear stationery; it's very easy to find. Ask guests to bring their favorite teddy bear or stuffed animal from childhood. (If they don't have a bear they should borrow one from their favorite little person.) At some point during the tea, have each guest tell the story of his or her bear.

Decorate the party area with toys (borrow some if you don't have children). If the season is right, pick a big bouquet of wildflowers, including dandelions, and place in a child's water glass. (Don't do this too far in advance; many wildflowers fade quickly.) Lullaby tapes (available in children's shops or baby boutiques) provide soothingly appropriate background music. If you have them, serve your tea in demitasse cups or even in tiny children's teacups. Keep the scale as small as possible.

For entertainment at your party, try reading some wonderful children's books aloud—a chapter or two from *Winnie the Pooh* can delight the most serious grownup child. After tea you might even want to play "pin the tail on the donkey," or you can just reminisce about your own childhoods. Be aware, though, that childhood memories might be painful for some people. If your guests seem reticent, don't probe; just try to make your teatime environment as safe and cozy as possible.

The menu for the teddy bear tea is designed to be simple, comforting, and reminiscent of childhood. Use your choice of ingredients for the sandwiches, but be sure to cut off the crusts, tea party style, and cut the sandwiches into little squares or triangles—however you liked them as a child!

Cinnamon-Apple Tea or Other Fruit Tea
Peanut Butter and Jelly Sandwiches
Oatmeal Cookies
Mama's Cinnamon Bears

CINNAMON-APPLE TEA

Any kind of herbal tea or
    mellow black tea such as
    Darjeeling or English
    breakfast
Clear apple juice
Sugar to taste
Cinnamon sticks

Brew tea using boiling apple juice instead of water. Use 1 teaspoon tea or 1 teabag per cup of juice. Pour tea into cups. Sweeten with sugar and stir with a cinnamon stick.

MAMA'S CINNAMON BEARS

These bears are based on my mother's wonderful sugar-cookie recipe.

1¾ cups sifted all-purpose
    flour
½ teaspoon baking
    powder
½ teaspoon baking soda
½ cup sugar
1 stick butter
1 egg
2 tablespoons milk
1 tablespoon vanilla
    extract
Sugar and cinnamon for
    sprinkling

Sift together flour, baking powder, baking soda, and sugar into large bowl. With pastry blender or 2 knives, cut butter into flour mixture until mixture has the consistency of coarse cornmeal. With fork, stir in egg, milk, and vanilla. Mix well with hands to form dough into a ball. Wrap in waxed paper and chill for 2 hours. Preheat oven to 350°. Lightly grease cookie sheets. Divide dough into 4 parts. On lightly floured surface, roll out each part to ⅛ inch thickness. Cut dough with bear-shaped cookie cutters. Bake for 7 minutes, or until golden, and sprinkle with a mixture of sugar and cinnamon. Cool completely. Makes 60 cookies.

Somehow, taking tea

together encourages an

atmosphere of intimacy when

you slip off the timepiece

in your mind and cast your

fate to a delight of tasty

tea, tiny foods, and

thoughtful conversation.

— GAIL GRECO

Tea to Go

A PARTY IN A BASKET

Tea is a portable feast and a wonderful vehicle for sharing. Here's an easily transportable tea party that can go visiting in the home of a friend or climb a mountain to enjoy the view. If you prefer, you can give the whole basket as a gift—with a teacup, a spoon, and all the goodies.

If you take your tea party to the park or to the beach, you will have to carry a portable stove or brew the tea ahead of time, strain it, and carry it in a thermos. Wrap sandwiches well and pack on ice in a small foam cooler or a thermal pack. Everything else will go easily in a large picnic basket, ready to enjoy.

Good Quality Teabags or Spiced Tea Mix

*Cream Cheese and Chopped Pecan Sandwiches
on Raisin Bread*

My Favorite Butter Cookies

Homemade Nut Bread with Three-Apple Apple Butter

SPICED TEA MIX

1 cup dry instant tea (can use decaffeinated)
2 cups dry powdered orange drink
3 cups sugar (may use half sugar substitute)
½ cup hot cinnamon candy
1 teaspoon ground cinnamon
½ teaspoon powdered cloves
1 package (about 1 cup) lemonade mix

Mix all ingredients and place in a covered container. Makes 1½ quarts. To give as a gift, pack in a small jelly jar with lid. Tie a ribbon across the neck with a bright plastic teaspoon. Also, include directions for mixing: one heaping tablespoon to one cup hot water.

MY FAVORITE BUTTER COOKIES

2 sticks unsalted sweet butter (softened)
1 cup sugar
1 egg, separated
1½ tablespoons Amaretto or ½ teaspoon almond extract
2 teaspoons grated orange zest
¼ teaspoon salt
2 cups flour
¾ cups sliced almonds

Preheat oven to 300°. Beat together butter and sugar until light and fluffy (about 3 minutes). Add egg yolk, Amaretto or extract, orange zest, and salt; beat well. Stir in flour and blend well. Spread and pat the dough evenly into a 10 x 15 inch jellyroll pan. Beat egg whites until foamy and brush evenly over the dough. Sprinkle almonds over top. Bake 40 minutes or until light golden brown. Cut into 2-inch squares while still warm.

THREE-APPLE APPLE BUTTER

This spread is delicious with raisin toast or any nut bread.

1 pound unsalted sweet butter
1 Granny Smith apple, quartered with core and skin
1 Winesap apple, quartered with core and skin
1 Macoun apple, quartered with core and skin
(You may use any combination of cooking apples, as long as some are tart and some are sweet.)

Place all ingredients in a heavy 4-quart saucepan. Cook 30 minutes over medium to low heat, lowering heat as apples cook and stirring occasionally. Force mixture through a sieve or stainless-steel strainer. Cool, cover saucepan, and refrigerate. Makes 3 cups.

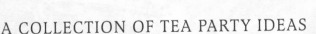

A COLLECTION OF TEA PARTY IDEAS

~ Enclose a teabag with your teatime invitations. Add a note inviting guests to enjoy one tea now and one tea later.

~ When serving a basket of scones or tea breads, sprinkle oatmeal and / or granola around the basket to create a smile of surprise.

~ Look for lovely old linens, trays, vases, cups, teapots, or spoons at garage sales or antique stores.

~ For a homey tea, set your tea table with an old or new quilt. The centerpiece could be an old hat from Grandma's trunk or a pretty bonnet. Have guests bring family photos to share.

~ Invite a friend to come for tea and bring along an unfinished craft project. After you enjoy your tea, play some soothing music, do your project, and talk.

~ For a sweet but different cup of tea, try adding a tablespoon of maple syrup to your cup. This would be a wonderful touch for an autumn tea—with decorations of colored leaves and bright apples.

~ It's fun to prepare your own tea goodies, but there's nothing wrong with buying them. Try a bakery, a deli, or a tea shop for delicious edibles. Then put your effort and imagination into setting a beautiful table and enjoying your teatime companions.

~ Enliven almost any tea gathering by having each guest bring his or her teacup. You will learn so much about each other as you talk about your cups. Some will be from wedding sets, some family heirlooms, some hastily purchased for the occasion.

As for social pleasures,

one of the highest enjoyments

is agreeable company and

good conversation; and

I especially like men,

women and children.

—WILLIAM
LYON PHELPS

Tea al Fresco

A SPRINGTIME
GARDEN TEA PARTY

A garden tea has to be my favorite type of tea party. I love to set up a pretty table out by our pond or on our patio or even in the tree house, pick a vaseful of beautiful blooms, and set out my most beautiful dishes. Somehow the tea and the food seems to taste twice as wonderful when enjoyed outdoors.

If you live in an area with no yard or garden, take your tea party to the park, or by a river, lake, stream, or beach, or even to the back of a pickup truck along the road. Just find a spot you like and enjoy.

Raspberry Tea

Egg Salad Sandwiches

Lemon Angel Food Cake

Chocolate Mints

*Scones with Mock Devonshire Cream
and Gertie's Apricot-Raspberry Jam*

RASPBERRY TEA

1 pot freshly brewed tea
    (any kind you like)
Fresh raspberries—3 to 5
    for each cup
Mint leaves and lemon
    slices (optional)

Brew tea according to the directions on page 9. Before pouring, put fresh raspberries in the bottom of each cup. Allow to sit for a few minutes to let the raspberry flavor permeate the tea. Or if you prefer, pour tea over raspberries in a pitcher and then serve over ice with mint sprigs and lemon slices.

EGG SALAD SANDWICHES

2 hardboiled eggs,
    chopped fine
½ cup mayonnaise
Salt and pepper to taste
1 teaspoon chives,
    finely chopped
8 thin slices white or wheat
    bread
Butter

Mix mayonnaise with eggs, chives, salt, and pepper. Spread each slice of bread with a thin layer of butter. Divide the egg salad among 4 slices of the bread; top with the rest of the bread. Trim the crusts and cut each sandwich into 3 parallel sections to make finger slices. Refrigerate or keep in a cooler until right before serving time.

LEMON ANGEL FOOD CAKE

This looks beautiful and is very quick and easy.

1 prepared angel food cake
3 ounces lemon pudding
    mix (not instant)
2 cups water
1 lemon for peel
2 tablespoons lemon juice
2½ cups heavy cream
14 ounces flaked coconut

Prepare pudding mix using 2 cups of water. Remove from heat and stir in lemon juice and peel. Pour into medium bowl, cover, and refrigerate one hour. Split cake into five layers. Whip 1 cup cream and fold into lemon filling with 7 ounces coconut. Spread evenly over each layer. Cover and refrigerate overnight. Whip remaining cream with ½ cup confectioners' sugar and vanilla. Frost top and sides using coconut for topping.

GERTIE'S APRICOT-RASPBERRY JAM

This recipe is from my husband's mother. Gertie makes the best jams, and this is one of my very favorites. I serve it at teas all the time and always get compliments!

2 pounds apricots (6 cups pared, pitted, and sliced)
¼ cup water
4½ cups sugar
1½ cups raspberries

Add water to apricots. Add sugar and raspberries and cook until jam is desired consistency. Pour into sterilized jars and seal while hot.

The cosy fire is bright and gay,

The merry kettle boils away

And hums a cheerful song.

I sing the saucer and the cup,

Pray, Mary, fill the teapot up,

And do not make it strong.

—BARRY PAIN

Before
We Meet

A STUDY GROUP TEA PARTY

How many meetings do you attend in the course of a week? Most of the people I know are heavily involved in church groups, PTA, discussion forums, civic organizations, or business networks. A simple or elaborate tea party can add a note of celebration to any of these gatherings.

If you are a member of a book study group, for example, why not begin your meeting with a tea party? Gather around the tea table first; perhaps the centerpiece could feature the book chosen for today's discussion. Then, if the setup permits, carry your cups and plates with you so you can sip and nibble while you talk. Brew another pot of tea midway through the meeting and pour another round.

Apple Tea
Almond Chicken Tea Sandwiches
Shortcake Biscuits with Clotted Cream
Sliced Fruit

APPLE TEA

Any kind of herbal tea or mel-
low black tea such as
Darjeeling or English break-
fast
Clear apple juice
Sugar to taste
Cinnamon sticks

Brew tea using boiling apple
juice instead of water. Use 1
teaspoon tea or 1 teabag per
cup of juice. Pour tea into
cups. Sweeten with sugar and
stir with a cinnamon stick.

ALMOND CHICKEN TEA SANDWICHES

3 boneless, skinless chicken
breasts, cooked and
chopped coarsely
½ cup slivered, blanched
almonds
½ cup mayonnaise
White or wheat bread

Mix chicken, almonds, and
mayonnaise. Butter well each
slice of bread. On half the
slices, spoon about 3 tablespoons of almond chicken
mixture. Top with remaining
slices. Stack three sandwiches
tall. Wrap in wax paper and

again in a slightly dampened
kitchen towel. Let filling set
for at least an hour. Unwrap,
cut off crusts, and cut into triangles. For a different look,
cut sandwiches in 2-inch
strips and set on a doily side-
ways, with the strips of chick-
en filling showing.

SHORTCAKE BISCUITS

2 cups all-purpose flour
1½ tablespoons sugar
1 tablespoon baking powder
1½ teaspoon salt
¼ cup unsalted sweet butter, cut
into 1½-teaspoon-sized pieces
and frozen
1½ cup plus 1 tablespoon heavy
cream
1 egg yolk
1½ teaspoon vanilla
2 tablespoons confectioners'
sugar

Preheat oven to 375°. Mix
together flour, sugar, baking
powder, and salt. Add butter
and blend in quickly, just until
the butter is broken into
pieces about the size of small
peas. Add 1 cup of the cream
and combine with a fork until
moistened. Immediately turn

out dough onto a lightly floured board and knead about ten times. (You want small lumps of the butter to be visible.) Roll out to a thickness of ¾ inch, trying to keep the dough in a square shape. Cut into 6 squares and transfer to an ungreased cookie sheet. Mix the egg yolk with the remaining tablespoon of cream and brush on biscuits. Then make a cream glaze by whipping the remaining 1½ cup of cream, vanilla, and 1½ tablespoons confectioners' sugar. Brush this over the yolk glaze. Sprinkle with the remaining confectioners' sugar and bake 15 to 20 minutes, until golden brown. Serve with fresh fruit or very good jam, clotted cream, or crème fraîche.

If of thy mortal goods

thou art bereft

And from thy slender store

Two loaves alone to thee are left,

Sell one, and with the dole

Buy hyacinths to feed the soul.

— PERSIAN POET
C. 1300

Teacups in the Office

A HEALTHY TEA BREAK AT WORK

If you work in an office, your colleagues and coworkers probably make up an important part of your world. After all, you see these people more hours of the day than you probably see your family! Every day you share the excitement and the stress of the busy workplace environment. Why not set aside a special afternoon to share a cup of tea together?

Every office is different, of course, so the specific arrangements for an office tea will have to reflect your particular setting. Perhaps you will want to invite members of your department to the conference room to celebrate a birthday. Or you can make everybody's day by setting up a tea service in the lunchroom and treating employees to a warming cup as they come for their breaks. There are many ways to accomplish your purpose of injecting a little loveliness into a busy workday.

If you want to include the entire office, why not make simple invitations to send via interoffice mail—or even e-mail?

memo: COME TO TEA WITH US ON FRIDAY!

On Friday afternoon:
ACCOUNTS PAYABLE
will be serving afternoon tea in the employees' lounge. Bring your own china cup and join us during your break time for refreshments and conversation.

If you will be serving many people, you may want to use pretty paper cups. But why not ask your coworkers to bring cups from home? You'll have the fun of seeing what everyone brings, and the varied patterns will add a nice homey touch.

Make your serving table as pretty as possible—cloth, flowers, candles, and tea service. This is one setting where the convenience of teabags may be welcome. I find that most people love herbal infusions such as cinnamon apple or almond, and if you use this kind of tea you won't need to provide milk.

The menu for this office tea is simple and easy to transport, and health-conscious office workers will appreciate its low calories and wholesome ingredients.

Fruit and Spice Herbal Tea
Mrs. B's Whole-Wheat Carrot Cake
Sweet Lemon Scones with Yogurt Cheese and Apple Jelly

MRS. B's WHOLE-WHEAT CARROT CAKE

2 cups whole-wheat flour (or use all-purpose flour for a lighter consistency)
1 tablespoon toasted wheat germ
1 teaspoon baking powder
1 teaspoon baking soda
1 teaspoon salt
1 teaspoon ground cinnamon
1¼ cups honey
¼ cup brown sugar
1½ cup unsalted sweet butter (melted)
1 teaspoon molasses
1 teaspoon vanilla
4 eggs
3 cups finely shredded carrots
1 cup chopped pecans or walnuts

Preheat oven to 350°. Grease and flour two 8-inch or 9-inch round baking pans. In mixer bowl combine flour, wheat germ, baking powder, baking soda, salt, and cinnamon. Add honey, sugar, butter, molasses, and vanilla; beat on low speed until combined. Add eggs one at a time, beating well after each egg, then stir in carrots and nuts. Pour batter into pans and bake 30 to 35 minutes, or until toothpick comes out clean. Cool on wire racks for 10 minutes, then remove from pans and cool completely before spreading with cream-cheese frosting. (You can also make in a bundt pan. When it is cool, dust with powdered sugar.) Serve in thin slices.

CREAM CHEESE FROSTING FOR MRS. B'S CARROT CAKE

8 ounces cream cheese, softened (use a "lite" version if desired)
1½ cup unsalted sweet butter
2 cups sifted confectioners' sugar
1 teaspoon vanilla
1½ teaspoon honey or molasses
¼ cup chopped pecans (optional)

In a mixer bowl, beat together cream cheese and butter until very fluffy. Then beat in remaining ingredients. Chill to spreading consistency.

SWEET LEMON SCONES

2 cups all-purpose flour
½ teaspoon salt
4 tablespoons sugar
1 tablespoon baking powder
3½ tablespoons butter
One 8-ounce carton lowfat lemon yogurt
2 eggs, separated
1 teaspoon grated lemon peel
3 tablespoons heavy cream

Preheat the oven to 425°. Stir together flour, salt, sugar, and baking powder. Using a pastry blender, cut butter into flour mixture until it resembles coarse crumbs. Stir together the lemon yogurt, egg yolks, and lemon peel. Add to the flour mixture and stir lightly with a fork. Add cream 1 tablespoon at a time until dough begins to clump together. Gather dough on lightly floured surface and knead just three or four times or until the dough holds together. (Do not overwork!) Pat dough into a rectangle about ¾ inch thick and cut with 2-inch round cookie cutter. Place scones on ungreased cookie sheet and brush tops with beaten egg whites. Bake for 10 minutes or until light brown. Serve warm. Makes approximately 16 scones. The scones can be frozen before baking. Place on cookie sheet in freezer until firm, then put into plastic bag and keep frozen until ready to bake. Add just a few extra minutes to the baking time.

YOGURT CHEESE

This is a nice lowfat alternative to clotted cream. Or you can add herbs or minced vegetables and use it as a spread for crackers and vegetables.

2½ to 3 cups plain or vanilla yogurt, set without gelatin, gums, or starch (check label)

Line a colander with a double thickness of cheesecloth and place colander in a bowl. Put yogurt into colander and cover with plastic wrap. Refrigerate overnight. The liquid will drain from the yogurt, leaving smooth solids. Throw away liquid and add seasonings, if you wish, to the remaining yogurt cheese. Makes 1 cup.

She was passionately
interested in everything I did.
She spoke with candor
and good grace.
Then, defying the reality of
crutches and straightened knee,
on wings of hospitality,
she flew to brew the tea.

— TOM HEGG,
A CUP OF CHRISTMAS TEA

A Cup of Christmas

A SPECIAL HOLIDAY TEA

Christmas is a special time for friends and family to gather together, and a Christmas tea offers a wonderful chance to celebrate your relationships and the season itself. Let your cup of Christmas tea be your special holiday gift to your friends, your family, and yourself.

Start early to plan your tea so you can approach your celebration with serenity instead of panic. (I always begin planning in October for a mid-December tea.) Find beautiful Christmas-themed note cards with no message inside to use for invitations. And have fun when it comes to planning the decor and the menu, the Christmas season offers so many wonderful possibilities. Take full advantage of all the wonderful decorating materials that are available—sparkling red-and-green fabrics, lush and fragrant greens, all kinds of candles. Load your table with a groaning variety of sweet and savory foods. And let your holiday message be one of abundant good cheer and memories in the making.

Almost any "Christmas party" food lends itself to tea-party fare. I like to take advantage of rich flavors and wonderful ingredients.

Spiced Russian Tea
Southern Pecan Cake
Fresh Blackberries or Other Fruit
Marscarpone or Brie
Assorted Christmas Cookies

End your time together by singing carols around the fire or reading aloud from a Christmas classic—O'Henry's *The Gift of the Magi*, for example, or Tom Hegg's *A Cup of Christmas Tea*. The Christmas story from the Gospel of Luke is the perfect way to put the whole season in perspective!

SPICED RUSSIAN TEA

Russian tea was originally imported to Russia from China by camel caravan and traditionally served from a samovar or large tea urn. Russians drink their tea with lots of lemon and sugar, but no milk.

6 teaspoons Russian blend or any good black tea
1 pinch cloves
1½ pints freshly boiled water

Place tea and cloves in pot, add water, and brew for five minutes before pouring. Add sugar and lemon to taste.

SOUTHERN PECAN CAKE

This wonderful flourless cake was served at a Christmas tea.

2 cups pecans (very fresh)
5 large eggs, separated
⅔ cup sugar
1 teaspoon vanilla or 1 tablespoon cognac

Preheat oven to 325° and grease and flour an 8-inch springform pan. Roughly chop 1½ cup pecans; set aside. Finely chop the remaining pecans; add to other nuts. (A food processor makes the